# OUR WORLD

## Learn all about the world we live in

# OUR WORLD

## Learn all about the world we live in

Steve Parker

Parragon

Bath New York Singapore Hong Kong Cologne Delhi Melbourne

Produced by Scintilla Editorial Limited, Chelmsford

This edition published by Parragon in 2008

Parragon
Queen Street House
4 Queen Street
Bath BA1 1HE, UK



ISBN 978-1-4075-2603-4

Printed in Indonesia

# Contents

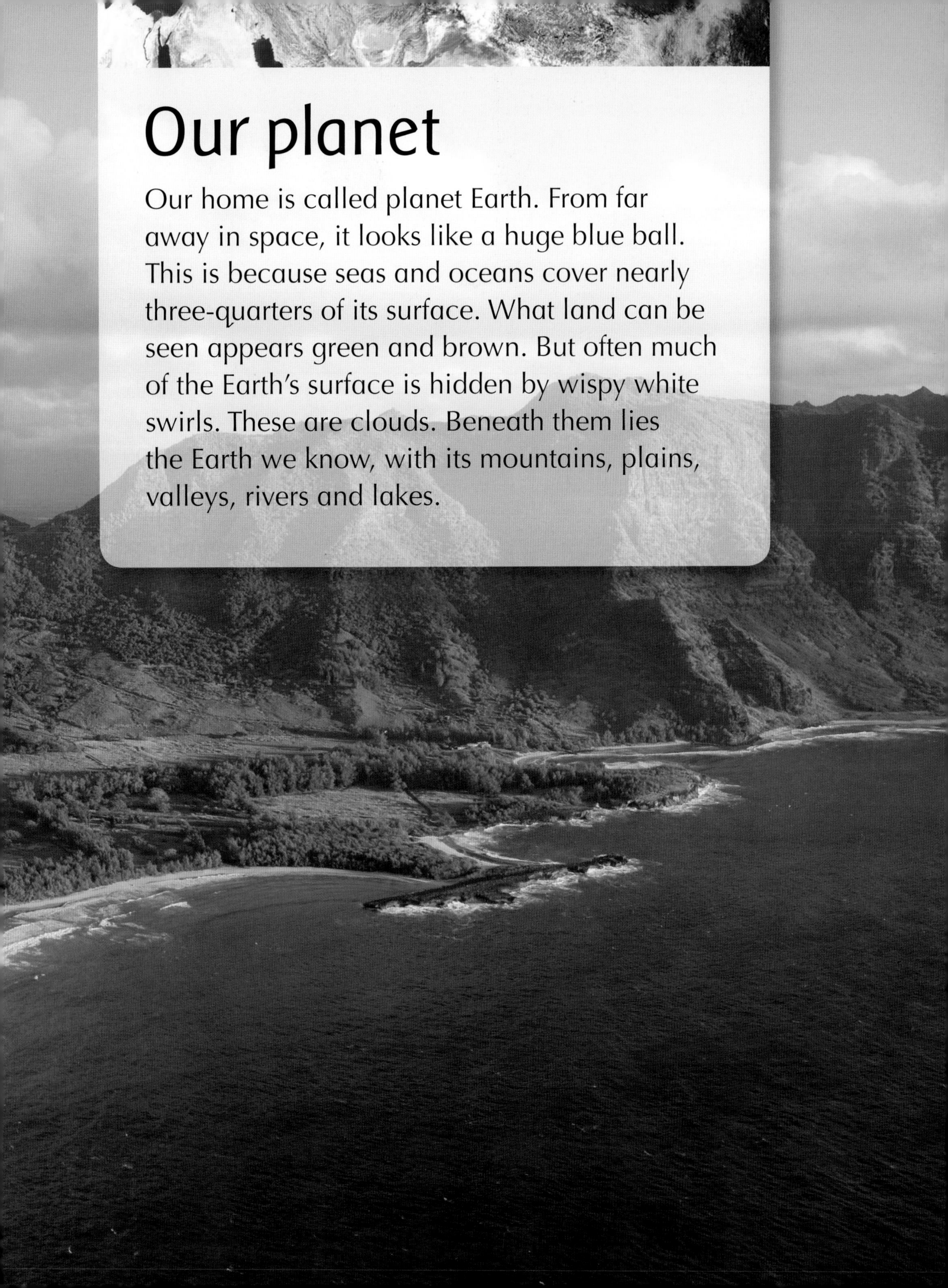

# Our planet

Our home is called planet Earth. From far away in space, it looks like a huge blue ball. This is because seas and oceans cover nearly three-quarters of its surface. What land can be seen appears green and brown. But often much of the Earth's surface is hidden by wispy white swirls. These are clouds. Beneath them lies the Earth we know, with its mountains, plains, valleys, rivers and lakes.

# Days and seasons

The ground we stand on seems still, but it is actually moving all the time. The Earth spins around once every 24 hours. This gives us day and night. The Earth also travels right around the Sun, once every year. This gives us the seasons.

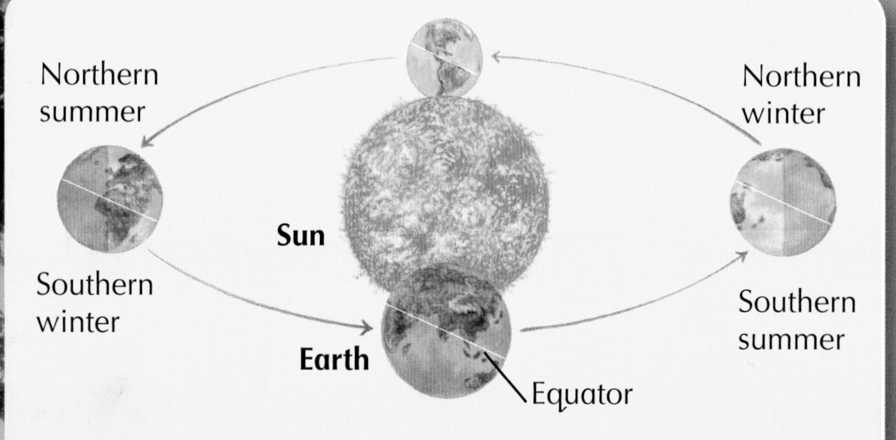


## Seasonal journey

The Earth travels at more than 150,000 kilometres per hour in its journey around the Sun. As it flies through space it does not spin upright, but is tilted at an angle. It is this tilt that gives the northern and southern parts of the Earth their summer and winter.

## The seasons

We have spring and summer when our part of the Earth leans towards the Sun. We have autumn and winter when our part of the Earth leans away from the Sun. The area around the middle of the Earth never tilts very much, so here it is sunny and warm most of the time.

## Cold at the top and bottom

The top of the Earth is the North Pole. The bottom is the South Pole. These places are the polar regions. Here it is cold all year, with lots of ice and snow.

## Sunrise, sunset

Every day the Sun seems to rise in the east, travel across the sky and set in the west. But it is really the Earth that is moving, not the Sun. Where the Earth turns to face the Sun it is daytime, and where it turns away from the Sun it is night.

## Hot around the middle

Around the middle of the Earth lie the Tropics, where it is always hot. Some tropical places are dry deserts. Others are very wet, and are covered by rainforests.

# Volcanoes and earthquakes

Earth's crust is hard, but inside is a swirling mass of melted rock. Volcanoes blast out smoke, ash and red-hot rock. Earthquakes can make the land shake so much that the ground cracks and houses fall down.

## Erupting volcano

When a volcano blows up, or erupts, it may make a tremendous noise. Smoke rises high. Pieces of rock shoot out, some as big as houses! Red-hot melted rock, called lava, pours out too. As the lava cools, it hardens.

## Deep under the ground

A volcano forms where hot liquid rock bursts up through a crack or hole in the Earth's surface. Sometimes the lava just pours out of the volcano and flows down its sides. But if the lava gets blocked, the volcano may explode in a huge cloud of dust and ash.

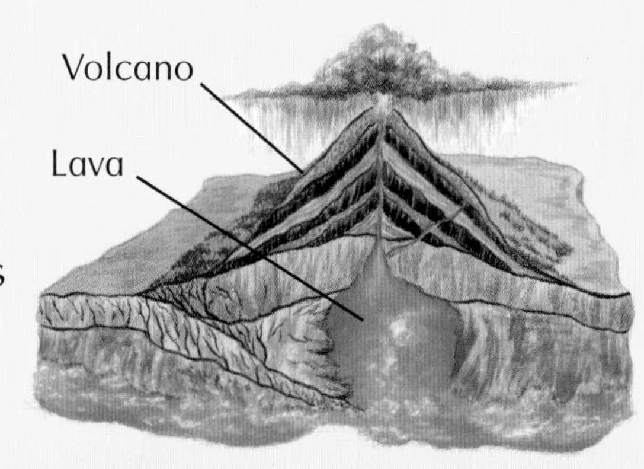

## Giant wave

Sometimes an earthquake at the bottom of the sea pushes up the water into a huge wave. When the wave crashes onto the shore, it can destroy whole towns. The giant wave is called a tsunami.

## Earth shaker

An earthquake makes the ground wobble like jelly. Buildings and bridges fall down, roads crack open and railway lines bend. Electricity wires, gas pipes and water pipes break. So there is great danger of electric shocks, fires and floods.

**DID YOU KNOW?**

If a volcano 'goes to sleep' and is inactive for many years, it is called a dormant volcano. But it may 'wake up' and explode at any time!

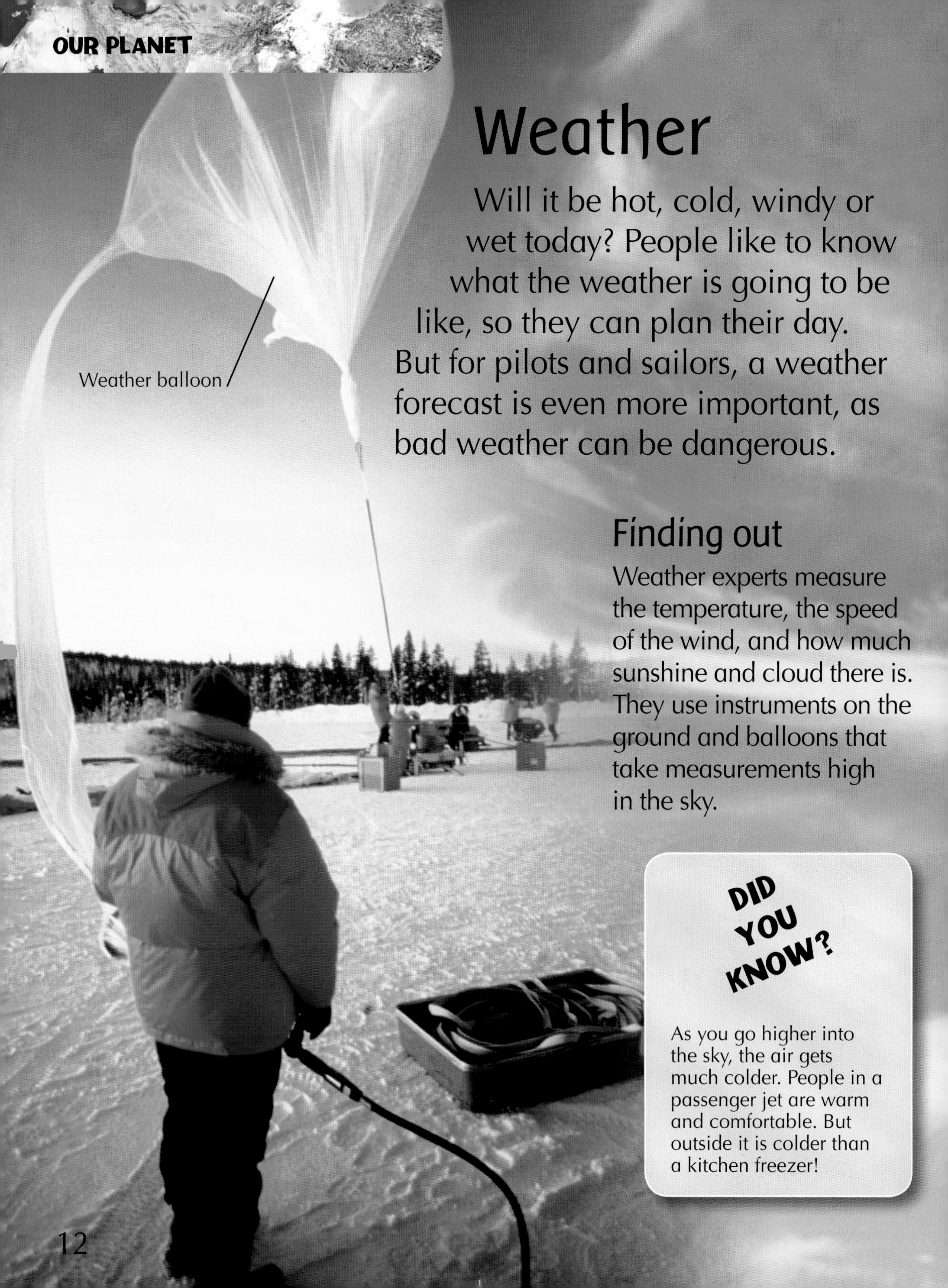


# Weather

Will it be hot, cold, windy or wet today? People like to know what the weather is going to be like, so they can plan their day. But for pilots and sailors, a weather forecast is even more important, as bad weather can be dangerous.

## Finding out

Weather experts measure the temperature, the speed of the wind, and how much sunshine and cloud there is. They use instruments on the ground and balloons that take measurements high in the sky.

### DID YOU KNOW?

As you go higher into the sky, the air gets much colder. People in a passenger jet are warm and comfortable. But outside it is colder than a kitchen freezer!

# Rain, hail and snow

Clouds are made up of tiny water droplets. When the droplets fall to the ground, we call it rain. If it is cold and the water drops freeze into balls of ice, it is hail. When they freeze into ice crystals they are called snow.

# Clues from clouds

We can often tell what the weather is about to do from the shapes and colours of clouds. If they are very high and thin, it will probably be fine and sunny. Low, dark clouds usually bring rain.

# Blowing

When air moves gently along we describe it as a breeze. When it blows very fast, it is a gale. If it gets any windier than a gale, it is called a storm, or hurricane. Winds this strong often blow trees over and cause damage to houses.

# Storms and floods

A big storm can be frightening. The wind howls, lightning flashes, thunder booms and the rain pours down. Some places have storms like this every few weeks.

## Spinning wind

A tornado is a small, fast-moving column of spiralling wind. It is wide at the top and narrow at the base. Inside the tornado, the wind often moves almost as fast as a jet plane.

**DID YOU KNOW?**

Some tornadoes are so powerful that they pick up bicycles and even cars. Objects are sucked up high inside the tornado, before being thrown out at the top and sent crashing to the ground.

## Thunder and lightning

A thundercloud is very tall, with a wide, dark base. Lightning is a giant spark of electricity, made when winds cause hail and water droplets in the cloud to bump together. The spark makes the air so hot that it explodes. This is the sound of thunder.

## Seen from space

High in space, weather satellites look down on the Earth. They take pictures of the clouds and weather below. The swirling cloud in this picture is a violent tropical storm called a hurricane.

## Too much rain

Some storms bring too much rain. If all the water cannot flow away down drains and along streams, it will flood the streets. Cars may be washed away and homes can be badly damaged.

# Mountains and valleys

The highest places in the world are the tops of mountains. Between them are low, deep valleys. Mountain slopes can be very steep. Sometimes rocks and boulders come tumbling and crashing down. This is called a landslide.

## Low down

Most valleys have a river along the bottom. The flowing water gradually cuts away the river bed and makes the valley deeper. Some valleys have steep sides and are called canyons or gorges.

## Deep, dark caves

Sometimes a river flows down a crack in the ground. Over thousands of years, it wears away the rock and makes a big cave. Some caves are so big they could swallow up the largest football stadium with room to spare.

## Shrinking mountains

Most mountains are millions of years old. But every year the wind, rain and ice slowly wear the rocks away. Tiny pieces slither and slide down the valley sides, where they are swept away by rivers. Slowly the mountain becomes smaller.

Some mountains are actually growing taller each year – even if only by a centimetre or two.

## On top of the world

The tops of mountains are usually cold and windy, and covered by ice and snow. They are often hidden in clouds. The highest mountain in the world is Mount Everest in the Himalayas. It is nearly 9000 metres tall – 17 times taller than the biggest skyscraper.

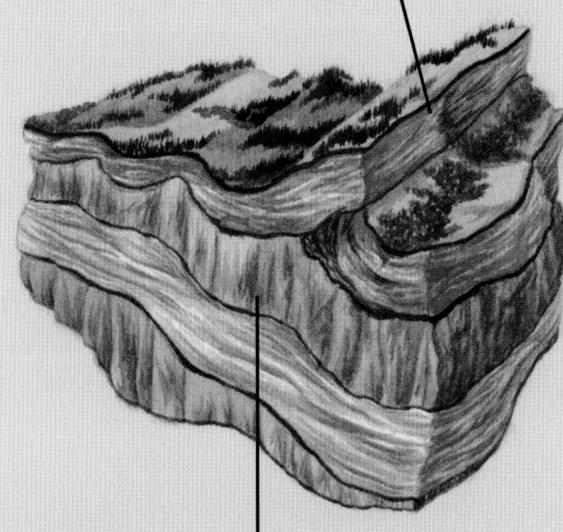


## Making mountains

The Earth's crust is made up of lots of rocky plates that fit together like pieces of a jigsaw puzzle. These plates move slowly over the Earth's surface. If they bump into each other, the rocks may crumple together and push up new mountains.

# Grasslands and deserts

Forests grow in places where there is plenty of rain. If there is less rain, grasses are the main plants. Where there is almost no rain, sandy or rocky deserts may form.

## No rain left

Deserts often form near mountains. The rain falls on high ground as moist air rises up one side of the mountain. There is little or no rain left for the lowlands on the other side, which turn into desert.

## Endless grass

Grasslands are wide and open, with just a few trees. The grass provides food for many different animals. The grasslands of Africa are called savannah, and they are home to elephants, zebra and wildebeest.

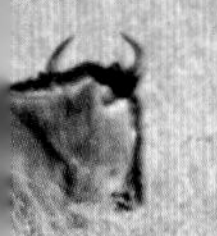

## Seas of sand

Some deserts are rocky, with boulders and stones. Other deserts are sandy. The wind blows the sand into tall piles called dunes, which look a little like the waves on the sea. It is very difficult to travel over the soft, slipping sand.

**DID YOU KNOW?**

The world's biggest desert is the Sahara Desert in North Africa. But the driest is the Atacama Desert in South America. In some parts of the Atacama, it has not rained at all for a hundred years!

## Plant survivors

Most deserts get very little rain, and only a few tough plants are able to grow there. Many desert plants have sharp thorns, or spines, to stop animals from eating them. A cactus stores water in its wide, thick stem.

# Woods and forests

A wood is a place with lots of trees and bushes. A forest is similar, but bigger. Woods and forests have lots of wildlife. Trees are home to many different animals.

## Mixed woods

Places with mild weather often have mixed woodlands of many different kinds of tree. You can tell the trees apart by their leaves, fruits and bark. Lots of animals, such as wild boar and deer, live in mixed woods.

## Cold forests

In the far north, it is cold and snowy for half the year. The most common trees here are conifers. They have needle-like leaves and often have branches that slope down, so the snow falls off easily. Animals such as caribou, wolves and bears take shelter among the trees.

## Tropical forests

Tropical rainforests grow where it is always warm and wet. Many rainforest animals spend all their time in the trees. Orangutans hang by their long arms and swing through the branches. They feed on fruit, leaves, bark and some insects.

## Wildfires

In very dry weather a forest might catch fire. This could be caused by lightning, or people being careless with matches! It can take up to a hundred years for the forest to grow again. Some plants have seeds that grow only after a forest fire.

### Redwoods

The tallest trees in the world are coast redwoods. Some of these amazing trees measure more than 100 metres high, which is taller than 50 adults standing on top of each other.

# Rivers and lakes

Where does all the rain go? It flows as water through drains, pipes and ditches, and into streams and rivers. These may carry the water to ponds or lakes, or all the way to the sea.

## Life of a river

A river begins where many small streams come together. It then begins a long and winding journey that usually ends at the sea.

Many streams begin as springs.

A tributary is a small stream or river that joins a main river.

## Rushing rivers

Rivers high up in the hills usually rush and gush over rocks. Some rivers have waterfalls. The water pours over a cliff, formed by very hard rocks, and splashes into a deep pool underneath.

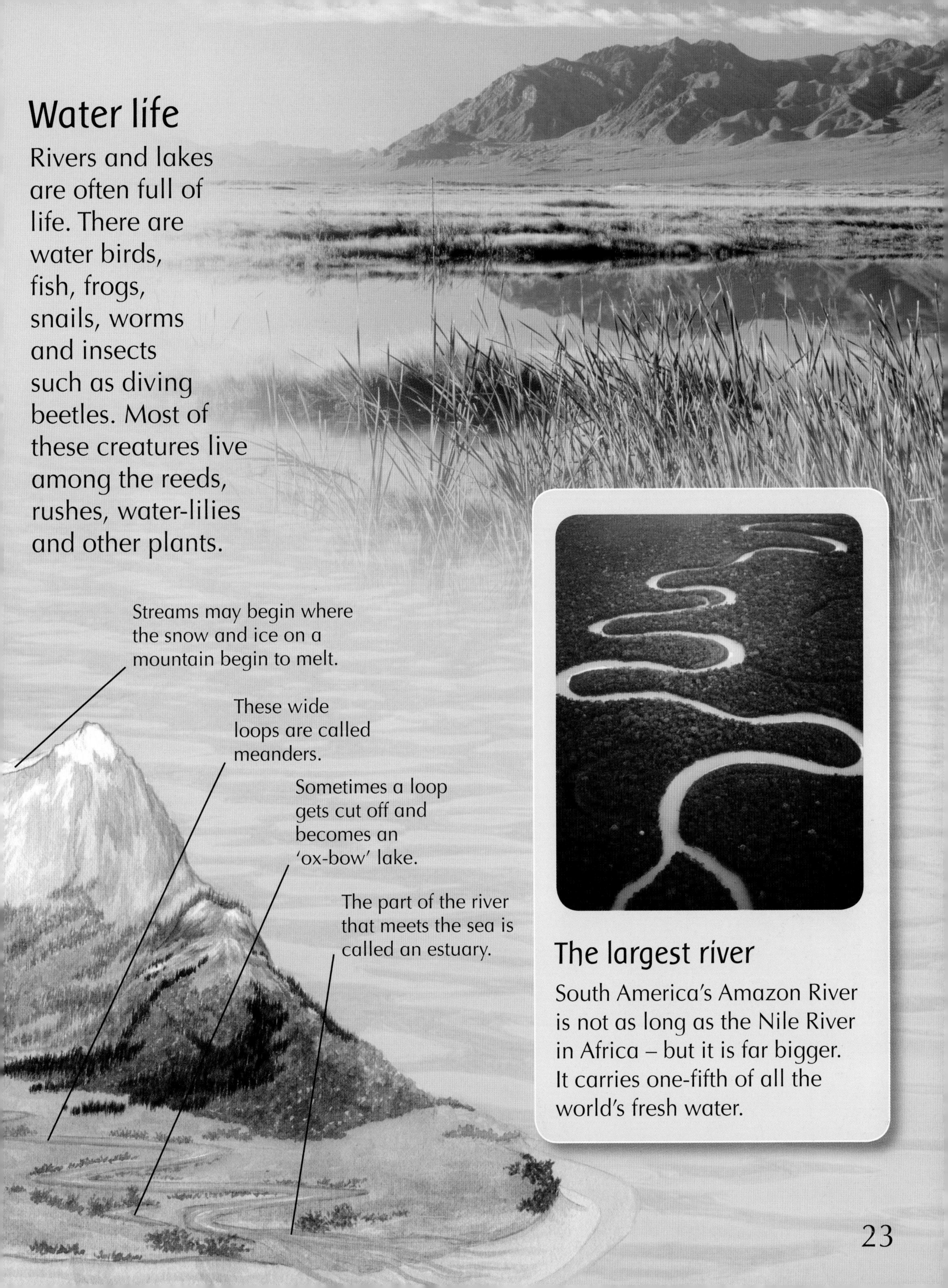

# Water life

Rivers and lakes are often full of life. There are water birds, fish, frogs, snails, worms and insects such as diving beetles. Most of these creatures live among the reeds, rushes, water-lilies and other plants.



## The largest river

South America's Amazon River is not as long as the Nile River in Africa – but it is far bigger. It carries one-fifth of all the world's fresh water.

# Seas and oceans

Almost three-quarters of planet Earth is covered by seas and oceans. This is why the Earth looks so blue when seen from space.

## Coral reefs

Where the water is warm, clear and shallow, coral reefs may form. Tiny coral creatures make little cups of stone around their soft bodies. When they die, more coral creatures do the same on top. Gradually the reef grows. Reefs also attract hundreds of colourful fish.

**DID YOU KNOW?**

The deepest place on Earth is the Mariana Trench in the Pacific Ocean near Japan. It goes down nearly 7 kilometres. The tallest mountain would easily fit into it and still be underwater.

## Silver shoals

Thousands of fish and other creatures live in the ocean. Some live around the shores. Others live out in the open water. Large groups of fish are called shoals.

## New islands

Beneath the waves, the seabed is a lot like dry land. There are mountains and valleys, deep caves and even volcanoes. Some undersea volcanoes grow so big that they break the surface and become islands.

## Under the waves

To explore the ocean depths, you need a submarine. This is because the deeper you go, the darker and colder it gets. The weight of all the water above also makes it difficult to move around.

# Earth in trouble

The Earth is rich in useful resources, from coal and oil to many kinds of metal. It also gives us water to drink and air to breathe. But we are using these resources up fast, and human activities are even changing the Earth's climate.

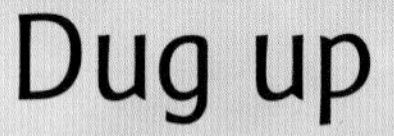

## Dug up

We dig up coal from deep mines underground and open mines on the surface. Some open mines are bigger than 100 football fields. All this digging destroys the landscape and the homes of wild animals and plants.

## Melting glaciers

Frozen rivers, called glaciers, are beginning to melt because the Earth's temperature is slowly rising. This extra water will make the seas rise higher and cause flooding.

## Saving water

Much of the water we drink comes from rain. But we also use water from underground lakes and wells that have taken thousands of years to fill up. Some of these wells have already run dry.

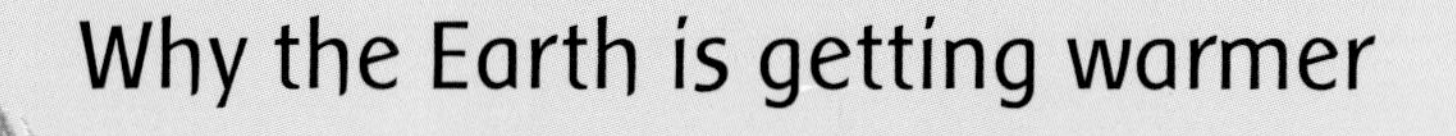

### Why the Earth is getting warmer

Sun's rays

Greenhouse gases trap heat in.

Only a little heat escapes.

Recently scientists have noticed that the Earth is getting warmer. They think this is being caused by 'greenhouse gases'. These gases, such as the carbon dioxide we make when we burn oil and coal, act like the glass of a greenhouse, keeping the Sun's heat in, and making the Earth warmer.

## Using oil

These 'nodding donkey' pumps bring oil to the surface from deep below ground. We use oil as fuel for our cars, and to make plastics, paints and thousands of other useful things. But if we are not careful, we will soon use it all up.

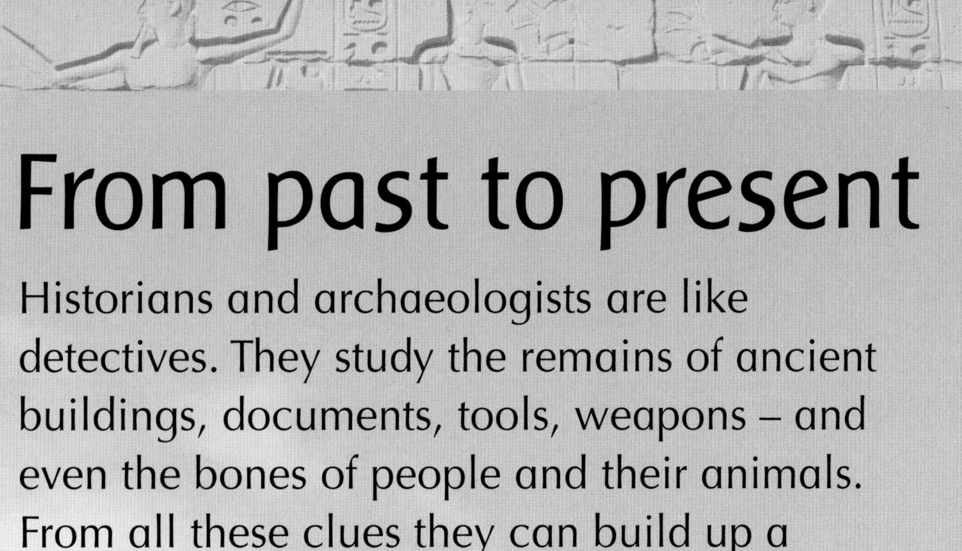

# From past to present

Historians and archaeologists are like detectives. They study the remains of ancient buildings, documents, tools, weapons – and even the bones of people and their animals. From all these clues they can build up a picture of what life must have been like a long time ago. They can also learn how the ideas and inventions from the past have helped make the world we live in today.

# Long, long ago

When our planet Earth began, there was no life. Huge storms with lightning, thunder and floods went on for millions of years. Rivers, lakes and seas filled with water. Then came the first living things.

Ammonite fossil

## Life begins at sea

The first living things developed in the sea. Ammonites had snail-like shells and soft bodies that looked like miniature squid. They searched in the mud of the ocean floor for food scraps.

## Life moves onto land

About 380 million years ago, some sea creatures began to wriggle onto the shore. Over millions of years, some of them changed and were able to walk and breathe air. Others, including the horseshoe crab, have hardly changed at all.

Horseshoe crab

## The dinosaurs

By 200 million years ago, dinosaurs ruled the land. Some were giant plant-eaters. Others were the biggest, fiercest hunters ever to walk the Earth. One of these, *Velociraptor*, had massive hooked claws to catch its prey. But 65 million years ago the dinosaurs died out.

## The Ice Ages

A few million years ago, the world became colder. Ice covered much of the land. Mammoths and other animals had thick fur to keep warm. These cold periods are now known as the Ice Ages.

**DID YOU KNOW?**

We find out about animals from long ago by studying their fossils. These are the remains of bones and shells that became buried and turned to stone.

# The first people

The first people gathered fruits and berries for food, and hunted wild animals. They moved about a lot, never staying anywhere for long. Then about 10,000 years ago they started to settle down in villages. They built huts, planted crops and began keeping farm animals.

## Cave paintings

About 30,000 years ago, people painted wonderful pictures on the walls of dark caves. The pictures showed animals such as deer, bison, long-horned cattle and horses.

## Early people

The Neanderthal people were a lot like us. They used fire and made tools and clothes. They even painted pictures on the walls of caves. But they died out about 25,000 years ago.

## Keeping animals

From about 10,000 years ago, people began to keep goats and sheep. Wild dogs were also tamed so that they could help people look after their animals.

### Stone tools

Long before people discovered metal they made tools from wood, bone and stone. A stone called flint was made into very sharp tools such as axes, knives and arrowheads.

Flint axe

## From caves to huts

Caves provided people with their first homes. But when people started living together in larger groups, they began to build their own homes from wood, leaves, stones and mud.

# The ancient world

The first great towns and cities were built in the Middle East and North Africa. The people who lived there invented writing and the wheel. They built temples for their gods and goddesses, and sent great armies to attack their enemies.

## Pyramid builders

The Ancient Egyptians lived along the River Nile in North Africa. They began to build their great stone mountains, called pyramids, about 4600 years ago. The pyramids were tombs for the Egyptian kings, who were called pharaohs.

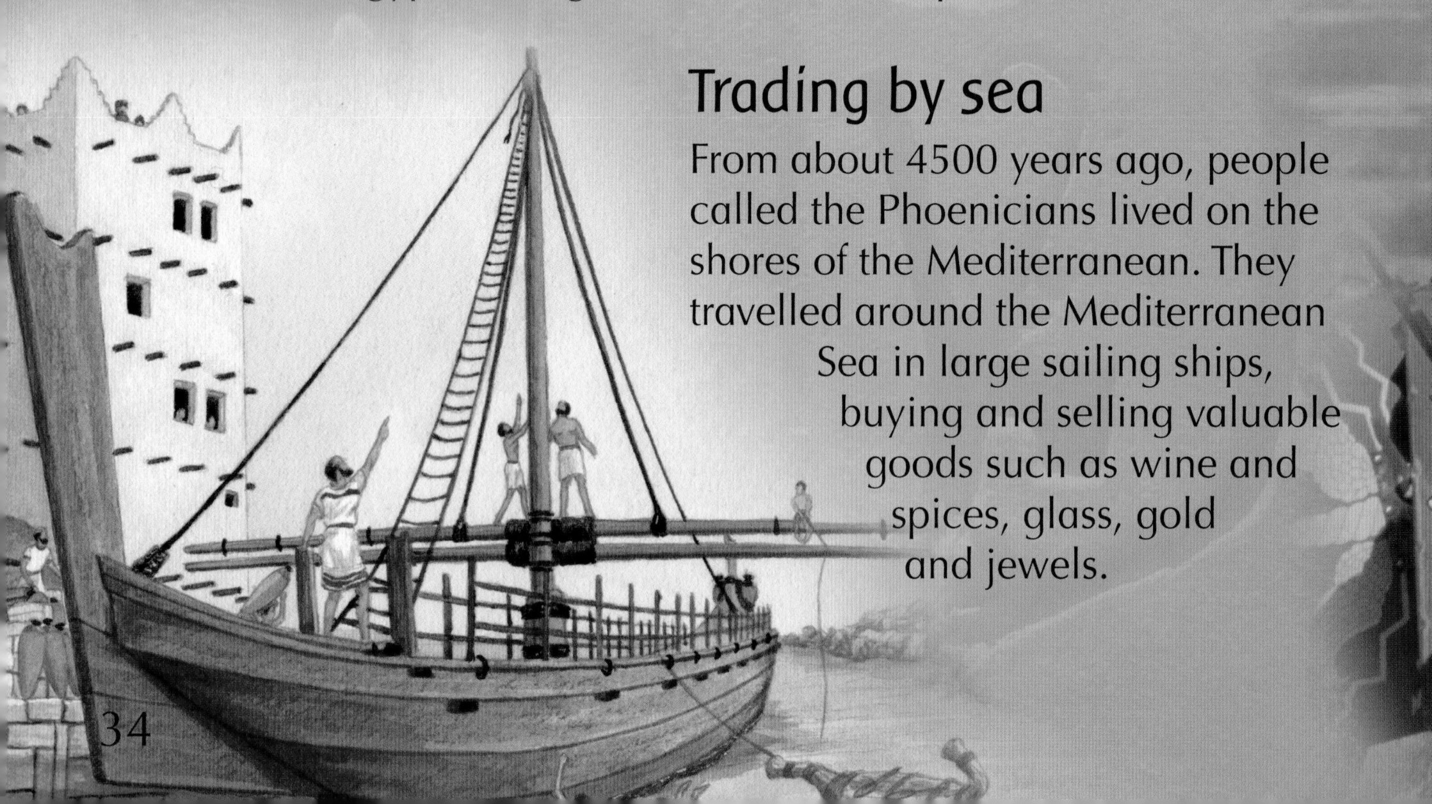

## Trading by sea

From about 4500 years ago, people called the Phoenicians lived on the shores of the Mediterranean. They travelled around the Mediterranean Sea in large sailing ships, buying and selling valuable goods such as wine and spices, glass, gold and jewels.

## Talented Greeks

Ancient Greece was very powerful 2500 years ago. The Greeks were not only great warriors, but also skilled in art, science and writing. Their style of building is still admired and copied today.

The Parthenon in Athens is a Greek temple built for the goddess Athena.

**DID YOU KNOW?**

The Colosseum is a huge stadium in Rome that could hold 50,000 people. Ancient Romans used to go there to watch fighters called gladiators battle to the death.

## A great empire

About 2000 years ago, the Romans had the best army in the world. The army was very well organized, with groups of 100 men each led by commanders called centurions. The army won many battles and helped the Romans build a great empire.

# Cities of the Sun

From 2000 years ago, Central and South America were home to a number of powerful civilizations. The people built huge palaces for their rulers and massive temples for their gods. Many of these peoples worshipped the Sun as their god.

## The Aztecs

In the 1400s, the Aztec people took over part of the country that today we call Mexico. They made beautiful cloth, baskets and bowls, and wonderful gold jewellery. To please their gods they killed animals and people in special ceremonies called sacrifices.

**DID YOU KNOW?**

Long ago, the peoples of Central and South America did not use the wheel. Everything was carried by people or by llamas.

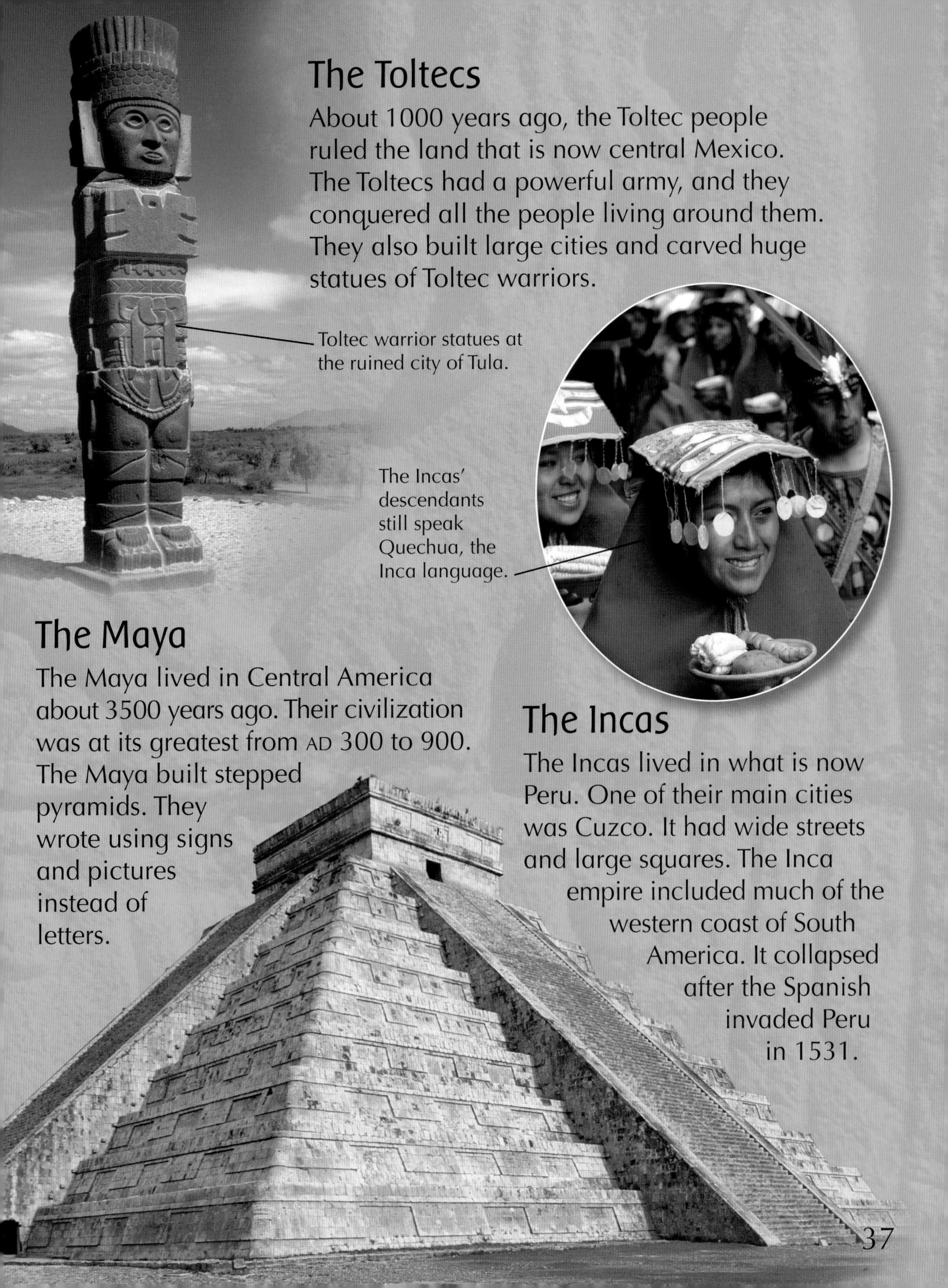

## The Toltecs

About 1000 years ago, the Toltec people ruled the land that is now central Mexico. The Toltecs had a powerful army, and they conquered all the people living around them. They also built large cities and carved huge statues of Toltec warriors.

Toltec warrior statues at the ruined city of Tula.

The Incas' descendants still speak Quechua, the Inca language.

## The Maya

The Maya lived in Central America about 3500 years ago. Their civilization was at its greatest from AD 300 to 900. The Maya built stepped pyramids. They wrote using signs and pictures instead of letters.

## The Incas

The Incas lived in what is now Peru. One of their main cities was Cuzco. It had wide streets and large squares. The Inca empire included much of the western coast of South America. It collapsed after the Spanish invaded Peru in 1531.

# Empires of the East

From about 1000 years ago, huge empires grew in eastern lands. Their rulers had great wealth and power, and fought many battles. Skilled people made beautiful pots, paintings and statues, and built many amazing buildings.

## Riding to war

The warrior king Genghis Khan led his people, the Mongols, in many battles. The Mongols rode fast and fought fiercely. About 800 years ago they ruled most of Asia, but their power soon faded.

The great temple at Angkor.

**DID YOU KNOW?**

Genghis Khan ruled one of the biggest empires the world has ever seen, yet he could not read or write.

## The Great Wall

Over hundreds of years, the Chinese built the Great Wall of China to keep out raiders from the north. It ran across hills and valleys for around 6000 kilometres. Today much of the Great Wall is in ruins, although some parts are in good condition.

## Shoguns

Japan was ruled by an emperor but most of the power was held by the top general, or shogun. There were many wars as important families fought each other for power and to become shogun.

## Largest temple

About 900 years ago the Khmer people of South East Asia built a giant temple at Angkor. With massive walls, over a kilometre long, and five huge towers, it is the largest religious building in the world.

# Knights and castles

Between 1100 and 600 years ago, many European kings built castles out of stone. Castles were designed to keep the people inside safe from attack. They often had thick stone walls, tall towers and protective moats of water all around them.

## Pretend battle

Knights were important soldiers who fought for their king. They sometimes practised their skills in pretend fights called jousts. They used a long spear called a lance, and a short sword.

### Cannons

As cannons became more powerful, the days of the castle came to an end. Firing stone cannon balls, these weapons could knock big holes in the castle walls.

## Well protected

A castle was more than a massive home. Often it was like a small village. Strong stone walls kept out enemies. Stores of food could last for months, and water came from a deep well.

## Life as a peasant

While the rich lived comfortable lives in their big houses or castles, ordinary people, called peasants, had hard lives. All their work was done by hand or using animals such as horses or cattle to pull ploughs or carry things.

# Exploring new lands

Since earliest times, people have been curious to explore new lands, where the customs and ways of life are different. Some explorers sailed the seas in search of riches or adventure, while others searched for better places to live.

**DID YOU KNOW?**

The Vikings chose the name Greenland to make people want to go there. In fact, Greenland is a much icier and colder country than Iceland.

## Across the Atlantic

In 1492, the Italian Christopher Columbus made his famous voyage of exploration to the Americas. He visited many islands in the Caribbean. On his voyage he took three ships with him, the *Nina*, the *Pinta* and the *Santa Maria*.

## Viking explorers

The Vikings of Scandinavia sailed their longships to settle in new lands. They became the first Europeans to reach America. Evidence of a Viking village dating back 1000 years has been found in L'Anse Aux Meadows in Newfoundland, Canada.

Travellers on the Silk Road today.

## The Silk Road to China

Long ago, only the Chinese knew how to make silk. It was brought to Europe along a route called the Silk Road. In 1271, an Italian merchant called Marco Polo took this road to China where he met the great leader Kublai Khan.

## The Maoris

There were no people in New Zealand until sailors from Polynesia arrived there just over 1000 years ago. New Zealand's Maori people are the descendants of these explorers.

Maoris performing a 'haka', a traditional war dance.

# The New World

America was known as the New World because most people from Europe did not know about it until Christopher Columbus went there 500 years ago.

## Native Americans

When the Europeans first arrived in the New World they found Native Americans already living there. Soon there were lots of battles as the Europeans wanted to take the land for themselves.

## Early settlers

People from Europe set up homes along the east coast of North America. As their numbers increased, they began to move west. They travelled in covered wagons with all their possessions.

## The wild west

The wide grassy plains of North America were so big, the farmers could let their cattle and horses graze freely. Each year the cowboys would round up the herds and take them to market.

### DID YOU KNOW?

The USA's capital city is Washington DC. It is named after a famous soldier from the War of Independence, George Washington.

## War of Independence

North America was ruled by Britain, but the people wanted to run their own country. They began a fierce battle called the War of Independence. In 1783, the Americans won, and the United States of America (the USA) was born.

The American War of Independence lasted over five years.

# A changing world

The 20th century was a time of great change. There were two terrible wars, in which many millions of people were killed. New technology altered the way people lived their lives. People also began to travel more, and enjoy more leisure time.

British Spitfire fighter plane

## The Great War

After many years of small battles in Europe, a bigger war started in 1914. This became known as the First World War. It lasted for four years, and more than eight million soldiers died.

## Air power

The Wright Brothers invented the aeroplane in 1903. By the time the Second World War started in 1939, the aeroplane had already become a powerful weapon. After the war, lots of people began to travel by air purely for pleasure.

## At the movies

The first films were made in black and white, and had no sound. But this did not stop comedians such as Charlie Chaplin becoming popular with people all over the world.

## The Ford Model T

By 1900, the first cars were on the roads. But they were slow and often broke down. The Ford Model T was the first car that ordinary people could afford to buy and that worked really well.

More than 15 million Model T Fords were made. Most of them were black.

## The Beatles

In the 1950s and 1960s, a new kind of popular music was made that appealed especially to young people. The Beatles from Liverpool became the best-known pop group in the world.

# The world today

History is what happened in the past. The important people and events of today will one day become history. It is hard to tell exactly what things will be remembered. It could be a terrible war, or discovering the cure to a deadly disease.

## High-tech cities

Countries such as China, India and Malaysia are developing fast. They are building new cities with all the latest technology.

## Shanty towns

Around many new and wealthy cities poor people live in shanty towns. Here, the houses are shacks, made from rubbish and often with no running water or electricity.

## Year 2000

A millennium is 1000 years. In the year 2000 people all over the world held parties and set off fireworks to celebrate the New Millennium.

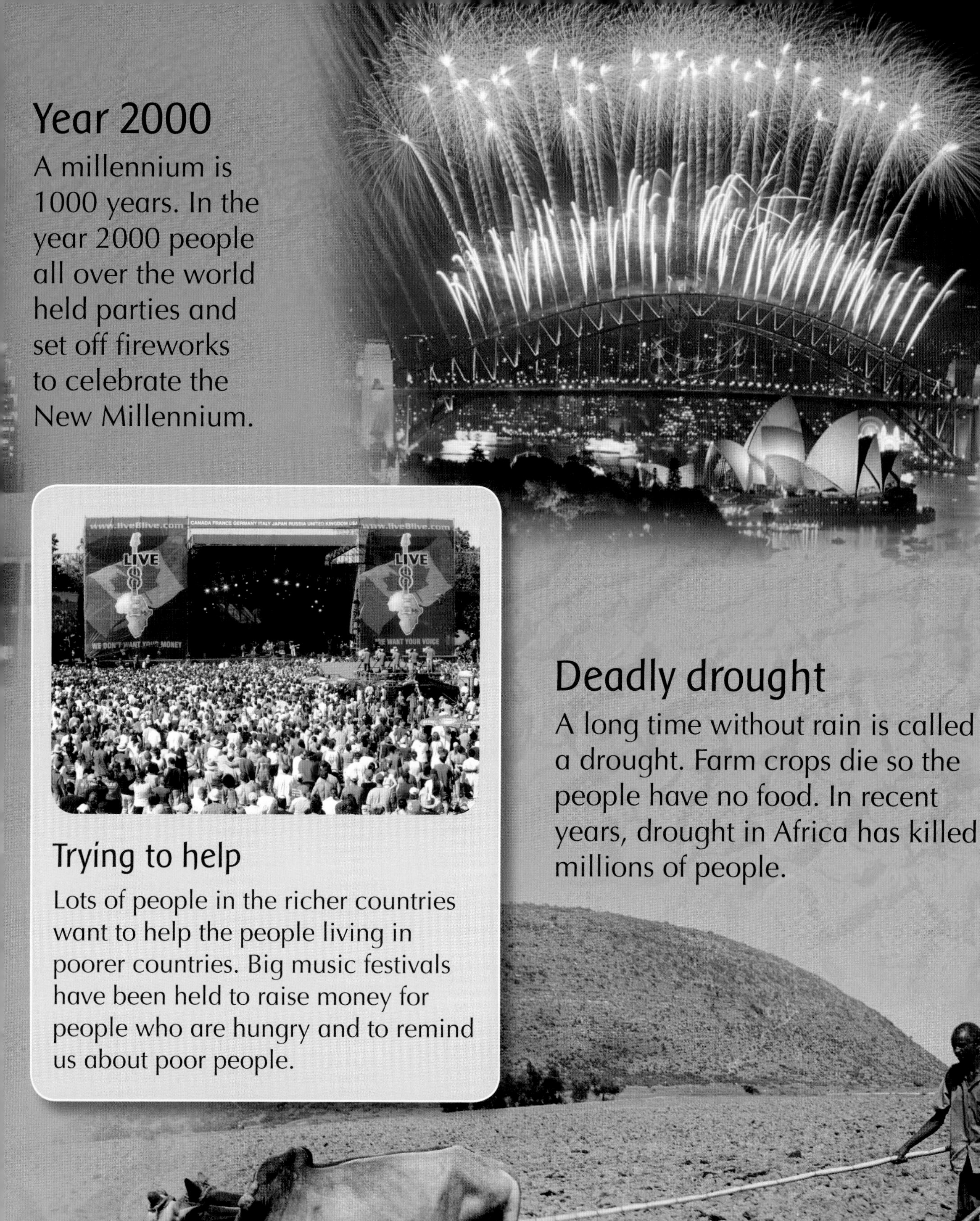


## Trying to help

Lots of people in the richer countries want to help the people living in poorer countries. Big music festivals have been held to raise money for people who are hungry and to remind us about poor people.

## Deadly drought

A long time without rain is called a drought. Farm crops die so the people have no food. In recent years, drought in Africa has killed millions of people.

50

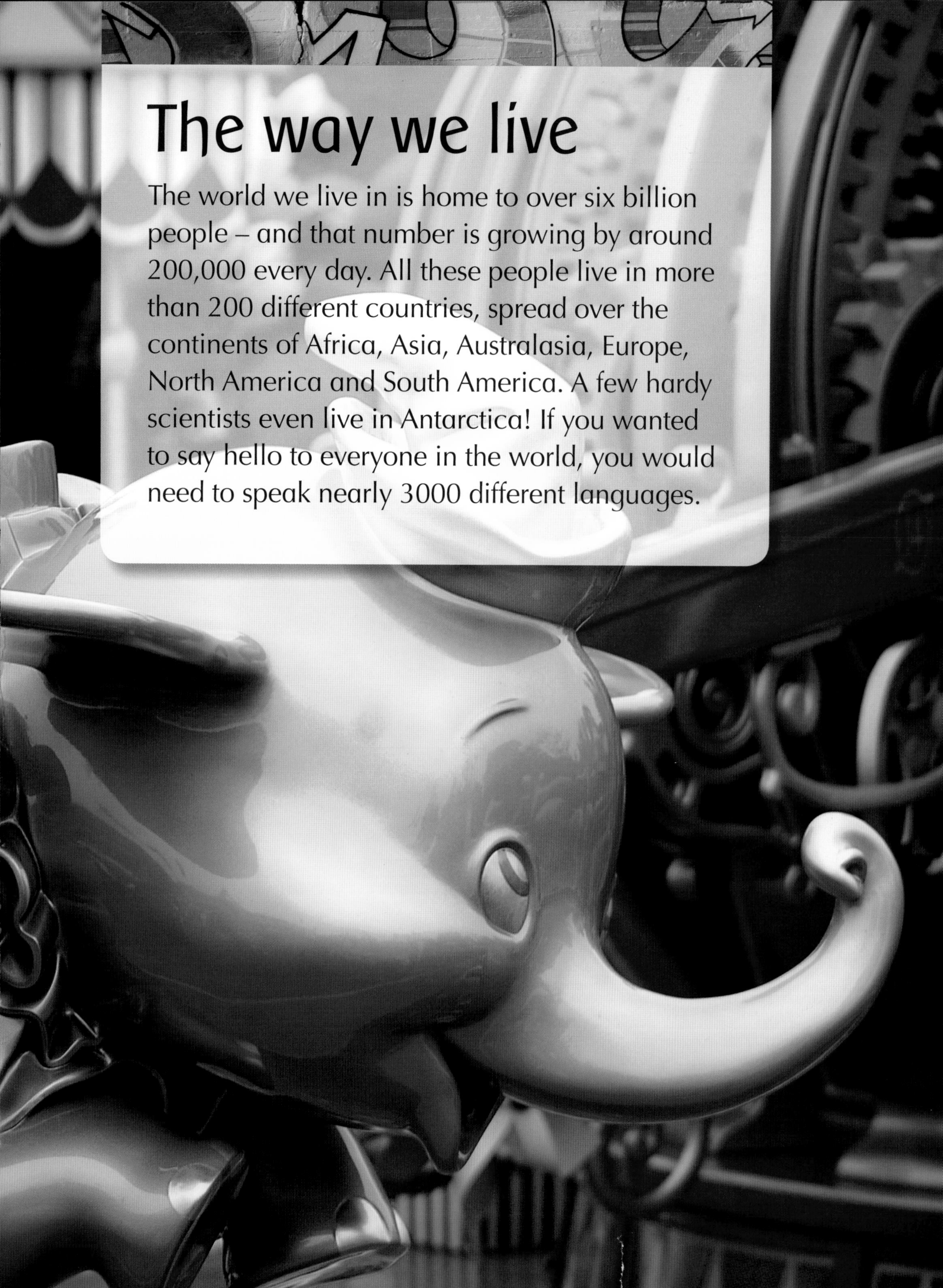

# The way we live

The world we live in is home to over six billion people – and that number is growing by around 200,000 every day. All these people live in more than 200 different countries, spread over the continents of Africa, Asia, Australasia, Europe, North America and South America. A few hardy scientists even live in Antarctica! If you wanted to say hello to everyone in the world, you would need to speak nearly 3000 different languages.

# The houses we live in

Around the world, people live in very different kinds of houses and homes. Some people live in high-rise city flats, others in tents made of felt.

## High homes

Cities are often very crowded, so many people live in flats or apartments. Some of these are in very tall buildings. Hundreds of people may live in one apartment block.

## Homes on sticks

In some parts of South East Asia, people build houses held up by strong wooden posts. This keeps the house clear of floods – and snakes. It also helps keep the house cool.

## Keeping cool

In hot countries, houses have plenty of shady areas to help people stay cool. Houses are often painted white. The white walls throw back, or reflect, the heat of the Sun.

### Mobile homes

Some people do not live in one place all the time. They are called nomads. Nomads usually live in tents that they can take down and carry. The nomads of Mongolia live in round tents called yurts. Yurts have a wooden frame, covered in felt, canvas and cotton.

## Mud houses

In Africa, houses are often made of mud. The mud can be spread over a framework of sticks and allowed to dry. But the mud can also be used to make bricks. It is pressed into brick-shaped boxes and dried in the sun.

# What people wear

Clothes may keep us warm or cool. Some clothes are very comfortable, others are smart or beautiful. Clothes can show that we belong to a particular group such as a school or a sports team.

## Shimmering sari

This beautiful silk dress comes from India. It is called a sari. It is one long piece of material that wraps around the body several times and drapes over the shoulder.

### DID YOU KNOW?

Silk is made by silkworms. These are really caterpillars of the silk moth. They spin a casing, or cocoon, of silk to protect themselves before changing into moths.

## Blue jeans

Jeans were created in the USA more than 100 years ago. They are usually made from a strong blue material called denim. Jeans were designed as work trousers for miners.

## Bright colours

In many African countries the clothes are often brightly coloured. They also have beautiful patterns and special stitching called embroidery. African clothes are usually loose and flowing, to keep people cool in the hot sunshine.

## Stay cool

For thousands of years, in the hot Middle East, people have worn long, loose robes. The robes are often white, to 'bounce back', or reflect, the heat of the Sun.

# At school

In most countries, children are allowed to go to school all year round. But some children have to stop school at certain times of the year to help gather crops from the fields.

## School clothes

In many schools, all the children wear the same kind of clothes as each other, called a uniform. This makes them feel part of the group.

## Outdoor school

In countries where it is hot, or the people are poor, school is held out in the open. The children may even sit on the hard ground.

## School bus

Children may walk or cycle to school, or go by car or bus. Often there is a special bus for school children. In snowy places they may ski or ride on a snow vehicle called a skidoo.

## High-tech schools

In many schools, children have lots of things to help them learn, such as computers or books. But in some countries, children have to share books, or have no books at all.

## Special schools

Some children go to special schools where they have extra lessons to learn how to dance or sing, or do sports. Other schools help people with special learning needs, such as deaf or blind people.

This is a special school for dance in Thailand.

# At work

People go to work to earn money so they can pay for their food, clothes and houses. Most people work only during the day, but others, such as doctors and the police, also work at night.

## In an office

Today, a lot of work is done in offices. People sit at a desk with a computer and a telephone. Computers are used for all kinds of office work, from writing letters and emails to doing really difficult sums.

## Skilled worker

Some people work with their hands to make or mend things. Carpenters work with wood, plumbers work with pipes, and electricians work with electricity.

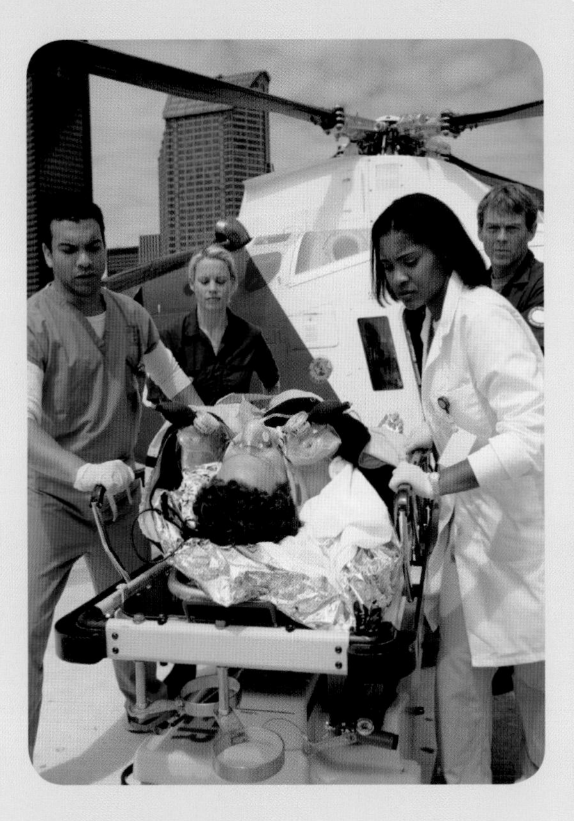

## Emergency!

Police, firefighters and ambulance crews are all part of the emergency services. Their work can often help to save lives. They must always be ready to help at any time of the day or night.

## Animal doctor

Veterinarians are trained to work with animals. Some vets need to understand how lots of different animals' bodies work. Other vets work with one type of animal, such as horses.

## In a factory

People who work in factories make things, or put things together, such as bicycles. Some of the work might be done by hand but a lot of it is done by machines.

# The food we eat

The food you see in shops and markets must first be grown as crops or raised as farm animals. In the past, people ate only what they could grow, catch or hunt themselves. Today, supermarkets sell food from all over the world.

## Preparing food

Food such as fish must be cleaned carefully ready for cooking. This fish has had its head, tail, scales and bones cut away. The fleshy parts that are left are called fillets.

## Steaming

In New Zealand, there are lots of hot springs and steaming geysers. These underground water sources are naturally hot. The Maoris use the water to cook their food and keep it warm.

## Eat in, take away

Today, people cook at home less often. We can go out to eat in a café or restaurant. Or we can buy take-away foods, such as pizza or burger and chips, to eat almost anywhere.

## Cooked over a fire

In some areas, people do not have electricity or gas. They cook meals in a big pot over an open fire. It can take hours to collect the firewood.

## Based on rice

In eastern countries, many meals include rice. Rice can be steamed and served with a hot, spicy curry, or made with milk and sugar into a pudding. In fact, some people eat rice for breakfast, lunch and dinner.

**DID YOU KNOW?**

One of the most costly foods is caviar. It is the tiny black eggs from a large fish called a sturgeon. The best caviar costs more than a new bicycle. It tastes very salty.

# Playing sports

Playing sports keeps you active and healthy. You can play as part of a team, or by yourself. Sports help people to learn about themselves. They learn how to lose without being upset, and how to win without being big-headed. Most of all, sports are great fun.

## Skiing

Skis allow you to slide over the snow really fast. Sometimes you can even jump through the air.

## Sport for all

Everyone is suited to some kind of sport – even people with disabilities. People in wheelchairs can play and enjoy a wide variety of sports, including archery, basketball and racing. Some wheelchair athletes compete in marathon races.

## Football

The sport that is played most around the world is football, or soccer. It is a team sport, with 11 players in each team. Every four years the best countries play against each other to try and win the World Cup.

**DID YOU KNOW?**

The biggest sporting event in the world is the Olympic Games. These Games happen every four years. Almost 4000 people take part in more than 25 different sports.

## Run and jump

Athletes who run short races very quickly are called sprinters. Sometimes sprinters have to jump over hurdles as well.

# Music, dance and art

Most people like to be creative in some way. They might like to sing, dance, play an instrument or paint. These activities are called the arts. You do not have to be good at the arts – the important thing is to enjoy them.

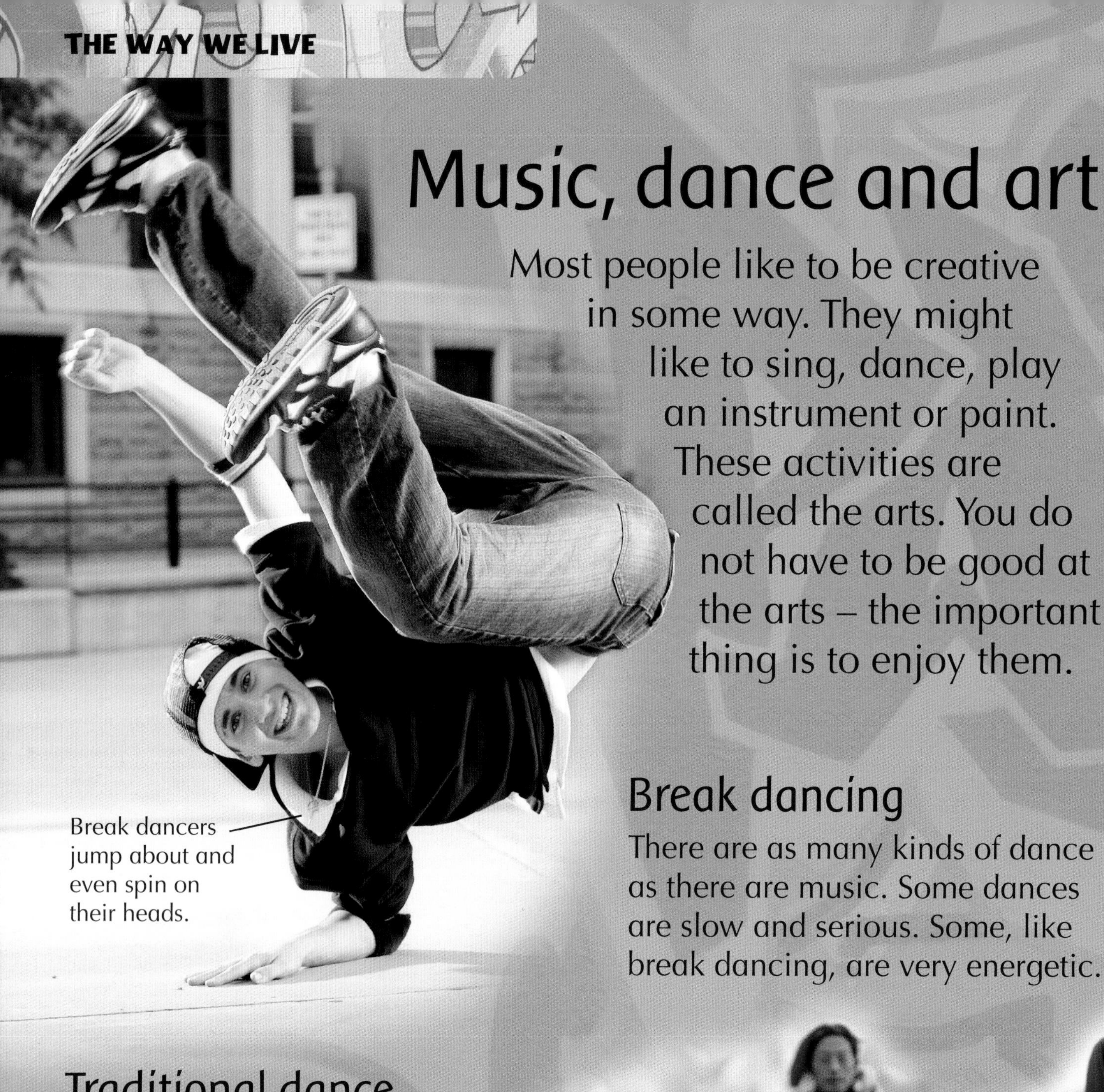

Break dancers jump about and even spin on their heads.

## Break dancing

There are as many kinds of dance as there are music. Some dances are slow and serious. Some, like break dancing, are very energetic.

## Traditional dance

Some types of music and dance are thousands of years old. These Tibetan dancers are performing at one of their summer festivals.

# Art everywhere

Ever since the first person drew the outline of an animal on a cave wall, people have loved to paint. A few paintings are so valuable they are kept locked up. Others help to brighten up drab city streets.

## Plan of a modern orchestra

A large group of musicians who play classical music is called an orchestra. Most orchestras have violins (1) and (2), horns (3), oboes (4), clarinets (5), flutes (6), bassoons (7), violas (8), cellos (9), percussion (10), trumpets (11), trombones (12), tubas (13), double-basses (14).

This statue is called the Strongman. It is in Japan.

# Sculptures

Many artists like to carve figures out of wood or stone. These sculptures can look very real. Around the world, sculptures can be seen in towns and parks as well as in art galleries.

# Running our lives

Most countries are looked after by a group of people called a government. It is the government that makes laws and takes big decisions such as how much to spend on hospitals, roads and schools.

Governments meet to discuss things in a special debating room.

## Lots of meetings

The government of a country meets often to talk, or debate, and make decisions. Usually there is one main leader who has the final decision. This might be either a president or a prime minister.

## Voting

In many countries people choose their leaders and the people they want in the government. They choose in secret and then post their answers in a special box. This is called voting.

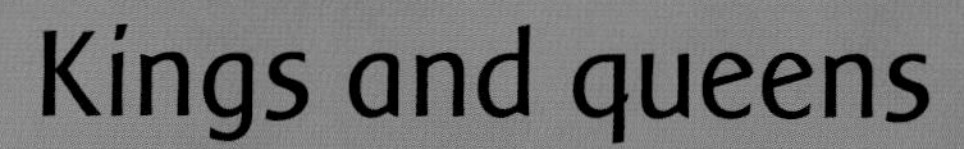

## Kings and queens

In some countries the leaders are kings, queens or emperors. They have power because they are part of an important family. Sometimes the government helps them to look after, or run, the country.

### United Nations

Almost every country in the world is a member of a big organization called the United Nations. It meets to sort out arguments between countries and helps when there are famines or earthquakes.

## Taking over

If there are great problems in a country, the army may take over. It makes new laws and keeps control. This is called a coup.

# Animals and plants

Life is all around us. Wherever we look, we see animals, plants and other living things. Animals are living because they grow, have babies and move about. Some of them burrow in soil or swim in water. Others run on the ground, slither among rocks, or fly in the air. Plants are also alive. They may not move about in the way animals do, but they grow and produce baby plants.

# Simple plants

There are millions of kinds of plants. They grow everywhere, from the tops of mountains to the seabed. Some are smaller than this letter 'o', others grow as tall as small skyscrapers.

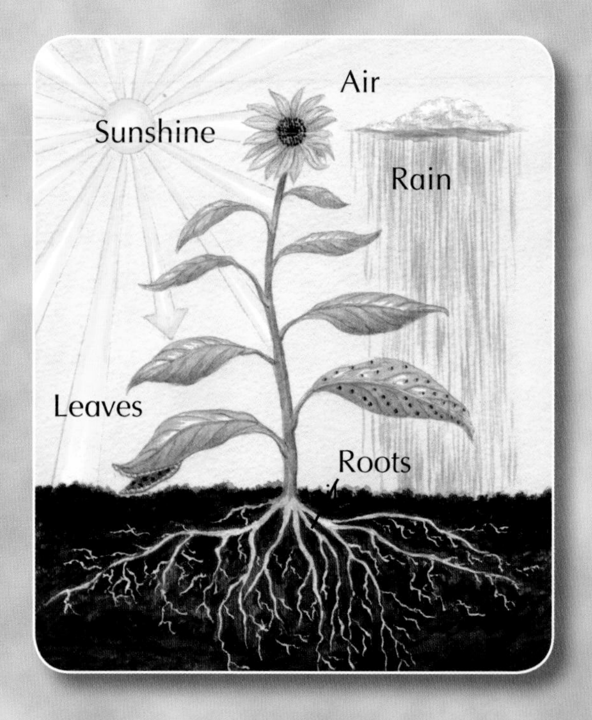


## Ferns and mosses

Ferns have wavy-edged fronds. Mosses have tiny green leaves. Both ferns and mosses like damp, shady places. Too much sunshine dries them out.

## Plants and growth

Plants must have sunlight and air to grow. They take these in through their leaves. Plants also need water and special foods called minerals. Most plants take these from the soil, through their roots.

## Seaweeds

Seaweeds do not have flowers and many kinds do not even have roots, but float in the sea. Some seaweeds are harvested for food. Others, such as wrack, are used to make toothpaste and ice cream.

Wrack seaweed

This stag-horn fern grows on trees.

## Air plants

Some plants do not need the soil to grow. Instead, they use their roots to cling to trees or other plants. These types of plants are sometimes called air plants. They get their water from dew and rain.

### Fascinating fungi

Both mushrooms and toadstools are types of fungi. Fungi are not plants but they are not animals either. They grow in damp places and feed on the rotting remains of dead plants and animals.

# Flowers

Some flowers are bright and beautiful, while others are tiny and hidden. Flowers help make seeds so that new flowers can grow. But the seeds cannot grow on their own. They need dust-like grains called pollen from another flower of the same kind.

## Buds and flowers

Flowers come out of small green buds. The coloured parts of a flower are called petals. In different flowers the petals can be white, yellow, orange, red, blue or even black.

### How poppies make their seeds

Seeds are made in the middle of the flowers. Pollen grains travel from one poppy and land on another. The part of the flower that contains the seeds then starts to grow and one by one the petals fall off. Holes open up in the seed pod and allow the seeds to fall out when the wind blows.

## How pollen moves

Some flowers let the wind carry their pollen to other flowers. But many flowers need animals to do this. The flowers make sweet nectar, which bees and other creatures love. As these animals drink the nectar, they get covered in pollen, which they carry to the next flower.

Dandelion seeds have fluffy parachutes that are carried by the wind.

## Spreading seeds

Some seeds are small and light, and blow away in the wind. Other seeds have tasty parts that animals eat. The animal drops the rest of the seed on the soil, where it grows into a new plant.

# Trees

Trees are the biggest plants of all. They are tall and strong, with lots of branches. They give us wood, fruits and nuts, as well as shade on a hot day.

Flowers, called blossom, open in spring and summer.

Trees that lose their leaves in autumn are called deciduous trees.

The main part of a tree is called the trunk.

Branches grow out from the tree trunk.

## Fruit

Much of the fruit that we eat grows on trees. Apples, pears and plums ripen in the autumn. Bananas and oranges can grow all the year round.

## Leaves in summer

In summer, trees such as the oak, beech and this fruit tree, have green leaves. But in autumn, when the weather becomes cold, the leaves turn brown and fall off. New leaves grow again in spring, when the warm weather returns.

## Leaves all year

Evergreen trees, such as the pine, have leaves on them all year round. Their leaves do drop off, but new leaves grow all the time. Pine leaves are long and thin, like needles. Pine tree seeds grow inside cones.

Pine cones carry seeds.

**DID YOU KNOW?**

When a tree is cut down you can see inside the tree trunk. Circles of wood start from the centre and grow out. If you count these rings, you can tell how old the tree is.

## Nuts

Many trees, including the hazel, walnut and beech, produce seeds called nuts that we like to eat. Oak trees produce nuts called acorns. People cannot eat acorns, but they are popular with squirrels and other woodland animals.

# Simple animals

Many animals have very simple bodies, without a bony skeleton. Some have no legs, while others have lots of bendy 'arms' called tentacles. Most simple animals are harmless, but a few can give you a painful sting.

The snail's eyes are at the end of these stalks.

## Sliming along

Snails leave a trail of sticky slime as they slide along. They come out at night when it is cool and damp, to eat leaves and other parts of plants.

## Living in soil

Earthworms live in the ground. They burrow their way through the soil and feed on any tiny pieces of dead, rotting plants that they come across. Earthworms are good for the garden, because the tunnels they make let air and rain into the soil.

**DID YOU KNOW?**

Simple animals do not have bones in their back. This means they cannot grow very big, unless they live in the sea. The giant octopus can grow up to 6 metres long and weigh more than 50 kilograms.

## Simple but smart

The octopus is probably the most intelligent of the simple animals. It can even open boxes and jars with its eight suckered tentacles.

## Jellyfish

The jellyfish floats in the sea. It can swim slowly by squeezing its umbrella-shaped body. The jellyfish trails its long stinging tentacles behind it to catch small fish and shrimps.

An octopus has eight tentacles.

Each tentacle has 240 suckers, which give the octopus a good grip.

Mouth

## Sea anemone

The sea anemone looks like a flower but it is really an animal. This ocean creature clings to a rock and uses its tentacles to sting small fish and push them into its mouth.

# Lots of legs

Some animals have six legs, or eight, or even more. Counting an animal's legs can tell us what kind of creature it is. If a minibeast has six legs, it is likely to be an insect. If it has eight legs, then it is probably a spider.

Tarantula

Swallowtail butterfly

## Eight legs

Spiders, such as this tarantula, have eight legs. Spiders hunt other creatures and kill them by injecting poison with their needle-sharp fangs. Some spiders chase after or jump on their prey, but others spin sticky webs to catch insects to eat.

**DID YOU KNOW?**

Crabs wave at each other! A crab has eight legs and two big claws. It waves its claws at other crabs to warn them to stay away or face a fight.

## Most legs

The animal that has the most legs is the millipede. Some millipedes have as many as 750 legs! Although they have lots of legs, millipedes move quite slowly. They like to munch on dead leaves and rotting wood.

## Many legs

The giant centipede lives in North America. It is speedy and bendy, and grows 30 centimetres long. It catches and eats cockroaches, crickets, mice and baby birds.

Giant centipede

## Six legs

All insects have six legs, and most have wings too. There are more insects in the world than any other type of animal, from scurrying ants to buzzing bees and beautiful butterflies sipping sweet nectar.

# Fish and amphibians

Fish have fins and a tail, and swim in water. The biggest fish is the whale shark of the open ocean. It is 12 metres long, which is as big as a bus. One of the smallest fish is the goby that lives in jungle swamps. This tiny fish can be as small as your fingernail.

Great white shark

## Ocean hunter

The great white shark is the biggest hunting fish. It has 50 razor-sharp teeth and eats fish, sea birds, seals and dolphins. Only rarely does it attack people.

Fish breathe using special parts, called gills, on the sides of their heads.

Many fish have a covering of hard, shiny scales.

Most fish can see well using their eyes.

Fins help fish to steer through water.

## Fast swimmers

Fish have smooth, 'streamlined' bodies that help them swim easily through the water. The sailfish can swim at over 100 kilometres per hour.

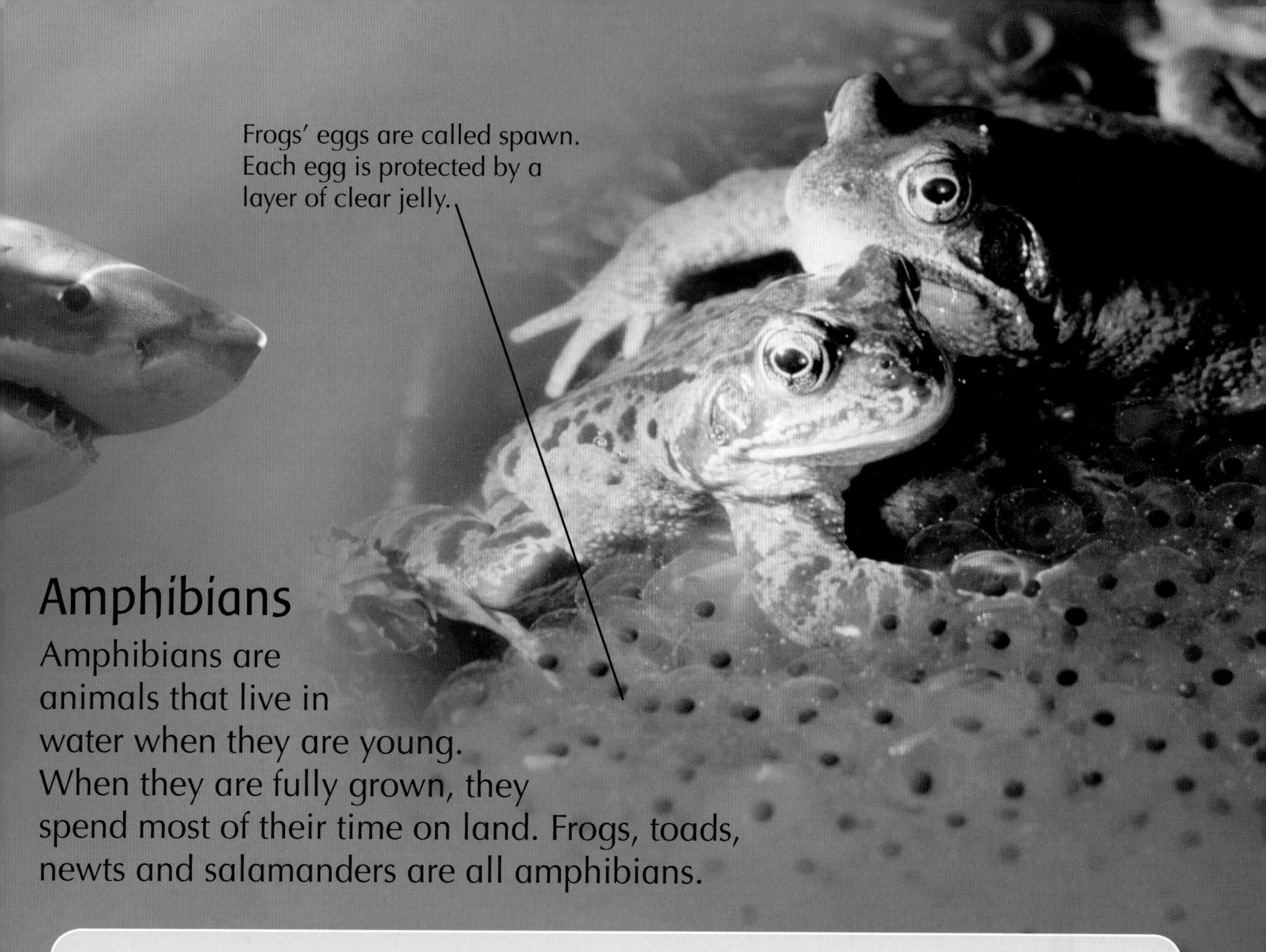


# Amphibians

Amphibians are animals that live in water when they are young. When they are fully grown, they spend most of their time on land. Frogs, toads, newts and salamanders are all amphibians.

## From frog spawn to adult frog

Female frogs can lay a lot of eggs, sometimes up to 4000. The baby frogs that hatch out are called tadpoles.

Young tadpoles have a tail but no legs. As they grow, the tail shrinks and their front and back legs appear.

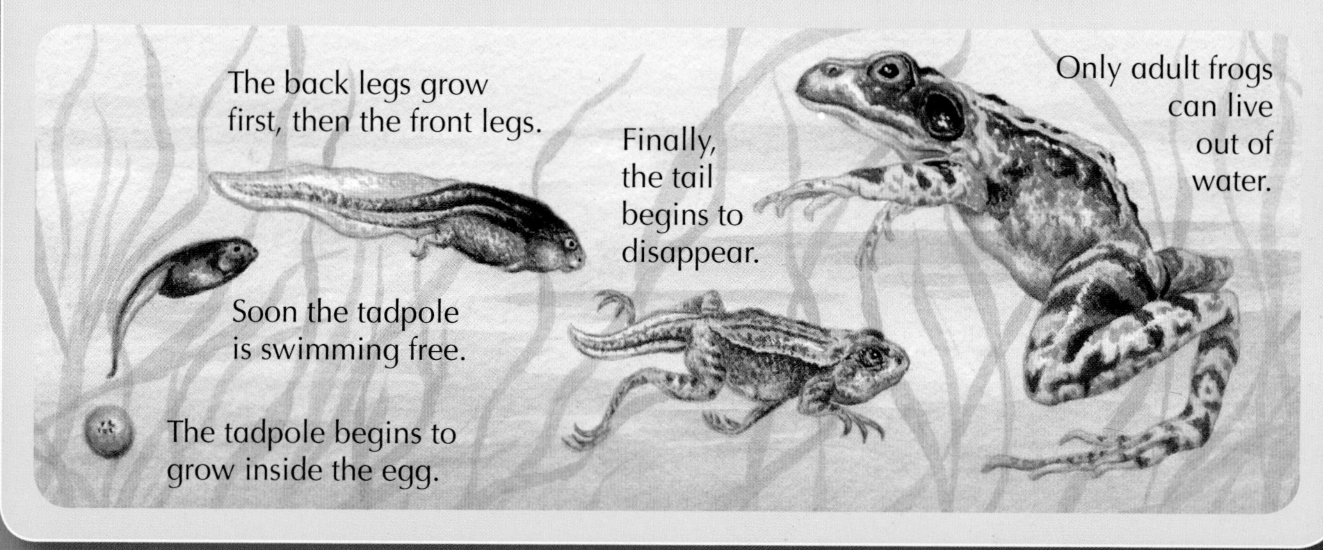

# Scaly reptiles

There are many kinds of reptiles. Lizards have four legs and can run fast. Snakes have no legs and slither quietly. Crocodiles and alligators are big, strong and toothy. Turtles and tortoises have a hard body shell. Most reptiles have scaly skin, and their babies hatch from eggs.

## Big bite

A crocodile hides in muddy water, waiting for an animal to come for a drink. When the animal bends down to take a sip, the crocodile grabs it with its huge jaws. Then it drags the animal under the water to drown it.

## Colour change

The chameleon is a lizard that can change the colour of its skin to blend in with its background. This helps it to hide from danger, and to ambush insects, which it catches with its long, sticky tongue.

## Danger on the beach

Female sea turtles lay their eggs on beaches and bury them in the sand. The baby turtles hatch and dig their way to the surface. They must hurry to the sea, or they may be eaten by crabs, gulls and lizards.

## Ready to strike

Snakes bite other animals using long, sharp teeth, called fangs. They cannot chew, so they swallow their meal whole. The cobra is a poisonous snake. It can flatten the skin on its neck, called its hood, and rear up to make itself look more frightening.

# Birds

Birds live all over the world, from jungles and deserts to the open ocean. They all have feathers, a beak, two legs for walking, and two wings for flapping. But not all birds can fly. Penguins use their wings to swim, and ostriches use their strong legs to run fast.

The bald eagle has a wingspan of around 2 metres.

## Big bird

The ostrich is the biggest bird of all. It is taller and heavier than an adult person. An ostrich cannot fly, but it can run faster than a racehorse. Its eggs are 24 times larger than a hen's egg.

## Eggs and chicks

Most birds build nests for their eggs. After they hatch, the baby birds, called chicks, open their beaks wide ready for food. The parent birds bring them food such as berries, flies, caterpillars and worms.

**DID YOU KNOW?**

Owls have such big eyes that they cannot roll them from side to side. But the owl can turn its head in almost a full circle to see what is happening behind.

## Flying high in the sky

A bird flaps its wings to push itself through the air. If there are warm currents of air, birds like the eagle can glide or soar without flapping. The eagle is a hunter. It has huge eyes to see animals far below.

## Good swimmers

Penguins live in cold southern oceans. They flap their wings to swim fast through the water as they chase food such as fish, squid and shrimps. Penguins lay their eggs and raise their chicks on land. Their thick feathers keep them warm even in the coldest weather.

# Mammals on land

Mammals are animals with fur that feed their babies on milk. Many pets and farm animals are mammals, including dogs, cats, rabbits, cows and sheep. People are mammals too. Mammals are warm-blooded. This means that they can move about and stay active even in cold weather.

## Flying in the dark

Bats are the only mammals that can fly. They also have such good hearing that they can fly in the dark. Some bats catch moths, mice or fish. Others feed on soft fruit.

Pronghorn antelope

## Mother's milk

A baby mammal feeds only on its mother's milk. Feeding on milk helps the young mammal to grow very quickly. It also means that the youngster must stay close to its mother, which helps to keep it safe.

## Fastest runner

The cheetah is the fastest mammal. It uses its speed to hunt other animals, such as gazelles. It can run faster than 100 kilometres an hour. But it can only do this for a short while, then it must rest.

**DID YOU KNOW?**

The elephant is the biggest land mammal. It weighs more than 5 tonnes – that is as much as 80 people!

## Looking out for each other

Many grazing animals, such as antelopes, buffaloes and wild horses, live together in large herds. This helps to keep them safe, because there are many more eyes to watch out for prowling wolves, lions or leopards.

# Mammals in the sea

Most mammals have four legs and a tail. But mammals that live in the sea, such as whales and dolphins, have fins and flippers instead of legs. Sea mammals must come to the surface to breathe air. Unlike fish, they cannot breathe under water.

Flipper

## Leaping out

Dolphins love to leap out of the water and splash back in. They chase after their food such as fish and squid. Dolphins talk to each other by making clicks, squeaks and squeals.

## Cow of the sea

The manatee is also called the sea cow. It munches underwater plants such as sea-grass, just like a cow eating grass on land.

## Fighting on the shore

Seals come ashore to have their babies. The biggest seal is the elephant seal. The males fight to rule over part of the beach. The mothers and babies must stay away from the fighting, so that they do not get squashed.

## Whales

The biggest whales, such as the humpback, have a mouth full of comb-like plates called baleen. They use the baleen to sieve out their food from the sea. Even though the whales are huge, they mostly eat tiny shrimps called krill.

**DID YOU KNOW?**

One difference between sea mammals and fish is the way they swim. Fish swish their tails from side to side. Sea mammals beat their tails up and down.

# Threats to nature

The biggest danger to nature is people. Around the world, people are hunting animals for their meat and skin, and damaging the natural places where plants and wild animals live.

## Too much rubbish

Every day we throw away huge amounts of rubbish, from old televisions to sweet wrappers. Much of it is harmful to nature. All this rubbish has to be taken away and either burned or buried in the ground.

## Fewer wild places

Every year there are more people in the world. They all need somewhere to live and food to eat. This means that more wild places are being destroyed so that houses can be built and food crops grown. It also means that there are fewer places for wild animals to live and wild plants to grow.

## Warmer world

We burn fuels in our homes, cars, factories and power stations. This releases gases into the air that make the world warmer. Global warming could melt the ice where polar bears live.

**DID YOU KNOW?** There are only 500 Sumatran rhinoceroses left. If people do not work hard to save them, they will soon all die out.

## Saving nature

Wildlife parks and reserves are special places set aside for animals and plants. Wardens protect the animals from hunters.

This rhino has been put to sleep so it can be moved to a wildlife park, where it will be safe.

# Some useful words

## Aquatic
Describes a plant or animal that lives in water.

## Carnivore
An animal that eats other animals.

## Conifer
An evergreen tree, like a pine, which makes its seeds in cones.

## Crater
The mouth of a volcano, or a bowl-shaped hole caused by an explosion or something hitting the ground.

## Crustacean
An animal without a backbone that has a body covered by an outer skeleton.

## Deciduous
Describes a tree that drops its leaves in autumn, and then grows a new set in spring.

## Desert
A sandy or rocky area where very little rain falls.

## Empire
An area or number of countries that are controlled by one person or government.

## Equator
An imaginary line that runs around the middle of the Earth.

## Estuary
A place where a river meets the sea and where salt water mixes with fresh water.

## Evergreen
A plant that has green leaves all year.

## Fossil
The remains of an animal or plant that have been buried for a very long time and become hard like a stone.

## Gills
The parts used by fish and some other aquatic animals to help them breathe under water.

## Global warming
The gradual increase in temperature of planet Earth caused by an increase in greenhouse gases.

## Greenhouse gas
A gas, such as carbon dioxide, that traps the Sun's heat and so helps to make the Earth warmer.

Herbivore
An animal that eats only plants.

Hurricane
A powerful storm with strong winds that often cause damage.

Krill
A small shrimp-like creature that forms the main food of some whales.

Lava
The hot, runny rock that comes out of volcanoes when they erupt.

Metamorphosis
A big change in body shape that occurs when some animals, such as frogs and butterflies, change into their adult form.

Mineral
A type of substance found in the ground, such as oil or coal. Also a substance needed in food to keep people healthy.

Omnivore
An animal that eats both plants and other animals.

Ozone
A form of oxygen found high in the atmosphere. Ozone protects the Earth from the Sun's harmful radiation.

Plankton
The tiny plants and animals that are found in ponds, lakes and seas.

Polar
Describes the areas around the North and South Poles of the Earth.

Pollen
A fine powder produced by flowers so that they can make seeds.

Prey
An animal that is hunted by another animal for food.

Satellite
A moon or a spacecraft that is in orbit around the Earth or another planet.

Skeleton
The bony parts of a body that support the muscles and other soft parts.

Tornado
A violent storm with winds that whirl around very fast.

Tropics
Areas of the world that lie around the middle of Earth, either side of the Equator. They are hot all year round.

# Index

# Acknowledgements


**COVER**

**Corbis:** TR epa/Robin Utrecht, TL Reuters; BL Matthieu Verdeil/Hemis/Corbis, BLL Maggie Hallahan; **iStockPhoto:** TC WorldWideImages; **Getty Images:** C Photographer's Choice/Jeff Hunter.

**ARTWORK**

**David Lewis Illustration:** 10BL Drew-Brook-Cormack,14BR Drew-Brook-Cormack, 21BL Drew-Brook-Cormack, 22TR Drew-Brook-Cormack, 26–27 BLBR Drew-Brook-Cormack, 33CL Drew-Brook-Cormack, 40BL Drew-Brook-Cormack, 47TR Drew-Brook-Cormack, 49CR Drew-Brook-Cormack, 53BR Drew-Brook-Cormack, 81CL Peter Visscher, 88TR Drew-Brook-Cormack, 90B Drew-Brook-Cormack, 99B Drew-Brook-Cormack.

**PHOTOGRAPHY**

**akg-images:** 40BR Hervé Champollion; **BigStockPhoto:** 13CL Joao Freitas, 69TR Giles DeCruyenaere, 69TL Giles DeCruyenaere, 72TL Giles DeCruyenaere, 74TL Giles DeCruyenaere, 76TL Giles DeCruyenaere, 76TR Razvan Photography, 77 aznatureArnon/Wilson Frisco, 78TL Giles DeCruyenaere, 78TL Giles DeCruyenaere, 82TL Giles DeCruyenaere, 84TL Giles DeCruyenaere, 86TL Giles DeCruyenaere, 88TL Giles DeCruyenaere, 90TL Giles DeCruyenaere; **Corbis:** 1C Kennan Ward, 2–3C Stuart Westmorland, 4T Rob Howard, 6-7C Danny Lehman, 8TL Zefa/Jorma Jaemsen, 8-9TRTL Kennan Ward, 9C Zefa/Farhad Parsa, 11BC Grant Smith, 12CL Saba/Shepard Sherbell, 13TR ANP/epa/Jasper Juinen, 13BR Maggie Hallahan, 16BL Archivo Iconografico, 20CR Stefan Meyers, 21CL epa/Miguel Vazquez, 21TR Zefa/Theo Allofs, 22CL James Randklev, 23T David Muench, 23CR Frans Lanting, 25TL Stephen Frink, 26TR Reuters/Alexei Kalmykov, 26B Ecoscene/Sally A. Morgan, 27BR Reuters/China Newsphoto, 28-29C Adam Woolfitt, 30BR Jeffrey L. Rotman, 34TL Gian Berto Vanni, 35B Charles & Josette Lenars, 36L Kevin Fleming, 36-37TRTL Paul Almasy, 37CR epa/Paolo Aguilar, 38TL Barry Lewis, 38-39B Dave G. Houser, 39BR Earl & Nazima Kowall, 40B Reuters, 41T Zefa/Peter Adams, 41CL epa/Syed Jan Sabawoon, 41 BR San Francisco Chronicle/Paul Chinn, 44C Brian A. Vikander, 44BR Dale C. Spartas, 46B Hulton-Deutsch CollectionHulton-Deutsch Collection, 47TR Sunset Boulevard, 47CR Reuters, 47BL Bettman, 48TR Casa Productions, 48BL Wendy Stone, 49TR Reuters, 49CL Mike Cassese, 49B Sygma/Les Stone, 50-51C Press-Telegram/Steven Georges, 53CL epa/Robin Utrecht, 53BR Peter Turnley, 55TR Michael Wray, 56TL David Turnley, 57CL Zefa/G. Baden, 58BR Stock Photos/Zefa/Lance Nelson, 59BR Louie Psihoyos, 60TL James Marshall, 60BR Wolfgang Kaehler, 61BR Liu Liqun, 62TL Zefa/Stefan Schuetz, 62BL Zefa/Herbert Kehrer, 62TR Zefa/Alexander Hubrich, 63B Creasource, 64BR Kazuyoshi Nomachi, 65TR Reuters/Gaby Sommer, 65BR Robert Harding World Imagery/Christian Kober, 67CL Reuters/Seth Wenig, 67TR epa/Royal Household handout, 67BR epa/Narong Sangnak, 70B Tom Bean, 71CL Sygma/Bernard Annebicque, 71R Michael S. Yamashita, 73TL Gallo Images/Anthony Bannister, 74BC Hans Reinhard, 74-75TRTL Herbert Kehrer, 77TC Brandon D. Cole, 77C Jeffrey L. Rotman, 78-79BRBL Gary W Carter, 80-81TRTL Tim Davis/DLILLC, 82B Martin Harvey, 82-83TRTL Tim Davis/DLILLC, 82CL David A. Northcott, 82TR Kevin Schafer, 84B Gallo Images/Peter Lillie, 85BR Royalty-Free, 86TL Theo Allofs, 86BL Mary Ann McDonald, 87T Tom Brakefield, 87B David Stoecklein, 88BL Daniel J. Cox, 88-89TRCL Craig Tuttle, 89TR Zefa/Ute & Juergen Schimmelpfennig, 89BR Brandon D. Cole, 90TL Francesc Muntada, 91T Ashley Cooper, 91B Gallo Images/Anthony Bannister; **Getty Images:** 9BR First Light, 10CL Science Faction/Jim Sugar, 14CL The Image Bank/Pete Turner, 14-15TRTL The Image Bank/Steve Bronstein, 15B Reportage/Radhika Chalasani, 16TC Discovery Channel Images/Jeff Foott, 17CR National Geographic/Gordon Wiltsie, 18BC James Warwick, 19 Photographer's Choice/Frans Lemmens, 20BC Nordic Photos/Kalervo Ojutkangas, 21BL Stone/Greg Probst, 24-25BBL Photographer's Choice/Jeff Hunter, 25BR The Image Bank/Cousteau Society, 32CR The Bridgeman Art Library, 35TR Photodisc Green/Adam Crowley, 37B Taxi/Michael Freeman, 39TL Stone/Christopher Arnesen, 52TL Photonica/Jorg Greuel, 52BR Robert Harding World Imagery/Upperhall, 53TR Stone/Manfred Mehlig, 54L Stone/Nicholas Prior, 55CL Stone/Lawrence Migdale, 55BR ArabianEye, 56BR Getty Image News/Robert Nickelsberg, 57TR Taxi/Gary Buss, 57BR Stone/David Hanson, 58TL Stone/Terry Vine, 59TL Photodisc Green/Ryan McVay, 59TR Photographer's Choice/Ron Levine, 61TL Reportage/Scott Nelson, 61TR Taxi/Rana Faure, 64TL First Light/Huy Lam, 66BL AFP/Lioel Healing, 66TR AFP/Kazuhiro Nogi, 68-69C Visuals Unlimited/Joe McDonald, 72TL Iconica/Andre Cezar, 73BR National Geographic/Joel Sartore, 78TL Photographer's Choice/Davies & Starr, 80BL Taxi/Peter Pinnock, 81TR Taxi/F. Millington, 84-85TRCL Image Bank/Riccardo Savi, 85TL Visuals Unlimited/Tom Ulrich, 90BR Stone/David Hiser; **iStockPhoto:** 7TR Stasys Eidiejus, 8TL Stasys Eidiejus, 10TL Stasys Eidiejus, 11TL Naphtalina, 12TL Stasys Eidiejus, 14TL Stasys Eidiejus, 16TL Stasys Eidiejus, 18TL Stasys Eidiejus, 19BL Jim Parkin, 20TL Stasys Eidiejus, 22TL Stasys Eidiejus, 24TL Stasys Eidiejus, 26TL Stasys Eidiejus, 27TR Yanik Chauvin, 29TR WorldWideImages, 30TL WorldWideImages, 32TL WorldWideImages, 32-33BG Michael Valdez, 34TL WorldWideImages, 36BG Stephan Hoerold, 36TL WorldWideImages, 38TL WorldWideImages, 40TL WorldWideImages, 40L Robert Creigh, 40-41BG Amanda Rohde, 42TL WorldWideImages, 44BG Danny Warren, 44TL WorldWideImages, 45TR WorldWideImages, 46TL WorldWideImages, 46-47TRTL Bas Rabeling, 48TL WorldWideImages, 51TR GWFlash, 52TL GWFlash, 54TL GWFlash, 56TL GWFlash, 58TL GWFlash, 60TL GWFlash, 62TL GWFlash, 64TL GWFlash, 66TL GWFlash, 71BL Ruud de Man, 73CL Jenny Horne, 75TR Rick Hinson; **NASA:** 5BR, 15TC; **Naturepl:** 75BR Brian Lightfoot; **Red Zebra Photo:** 41BL Gerald Peachey; **Science Photo Library:** 32BL Field Museum Chicago/Tom McHugh, 33CL Steve Gschmeissner, 33TR E. Hanumantha Rao, 33BR Tom McHugh, 76BL E.R Degginger, 79TC Gusto, 79CR Larry Miller; **The Natural History Museum London:** 30TL Dinosaurs & Extinct Species/Paul D. Taylor and David N. Lewis, 330-31TRTL Dinosaurs & Extinct Species, 31BR Dinosaurs & Extinct Species/Michael Long.